# Drumbeat

By Joy Cowley

Illustrated by Shane Marsh

Dominie Press, Inc.

Publisher: Christine Yuen
Editor: John S. F. Graham
Designer: Lois Stanfield
Illustrator: Shane Marsh

Published by:

🦔 **Dominie Press, Inc.**

1949 Kellogg Avenue
Carlsbad, California 92008 USA

www.dominie.com

Paperback ISBN 0-7685-1068-6
Library Bound Edition ISBN 0-7685-1484-3
Printed in Singapore by PH Productions Pte Ltd
    3 4 5 6 PH 04 03

# Table of Contents

# Chapter One

# The Farm

The year was 1864.
The place was a small farm
in South Carolina.

There was no cotton that year,
and not much food
for Joshua and Mary Beth
and their Momma.

The Union soldiers
had taken their milking cow
and their fattened hogs.
Now Momma was cooking
the hog's corn for the children
so they wouldn't starve.

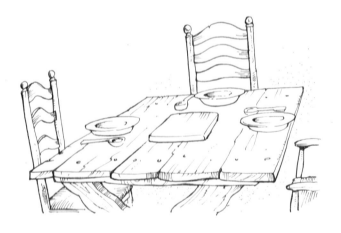

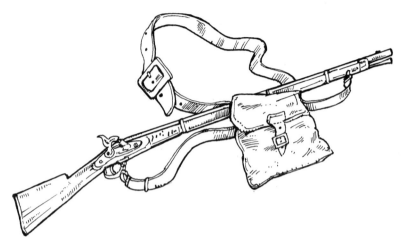

Momma didn't talk much.
She was worried sick
about their Poppa,
who was in the
Confederate Army.
He was fighting the Union
up north in Virginia.

Sometimes,
Joshua and Mary Beth
could hear guns going off.

Momma hugged them.
"Don't be afraid," she said.
"That old noise isn't guns.
That's just the beat of big drums."

But Joshua and Mary Beth
knew better.

## Chapter Two

# The Squeaking Barn Door

One moonlit night,
Joshua heard a noise
that made him jump awake.

It was the slow squeaking
of their old barn door.

Now, Joshua knew
he had bolted that door.

He ran to his window
and looked out at the barn.
The door was slowly moving.
Someone was inside.

Joshua ran to Mary Beth's room.
She, too, was at her window.

"Should we wake up Momma?"
Joshua asked.

"No," said Mary Beth.
"Let's go and look."

## Chapter Three

# **Around Back**

**B**y the back porch,
Joshua picked up the hay fork,
and Mary Beth found a strong stick.
They crept across the grass.

Maybe it was a wild critter
in the barn, and maybe it wasn't.

They didn't go in the big door.
That would squeak too much.
They went around the back
through the empty stable.
In the moonlight,
the barn looked about the same
as always—some loose hay,
some saws, the wooden plow.

But now there was a noise
that made them go cold.
Someone in the barn was crying,
a moaning kind of cry.

"Who's there?" said Mary Beth,
holding up her stick.

## Chapter Four

# A Friend or an Enemy

There was a movement
in the hay.
"Don't shoot! Don't shoot!"
cried a frightened voice.

Joshua said, "That depends on
whether you're a friend or an enemy."

"We don't have guns,"
said Mary Beth.
"But we can protect ourselves
if we need to. Just tell us why
you're hiding in our barn."

There was more rustling,
and a boy sat up.
"My leg's busted," he said.
"I can't walk."

"How old are you?" Mary Beth asked.

"Fifteen years," he said.

Mary Beth turned to Joshua.
"Go and wake Momma," she said.

Chapter Five

# The Uniform

**W**hen Momma came in
with the lantern,
the first thing they saw
was the boy's uniform.
He was a Union soldier.

The second thing they saw
was the blood.
His leg was a real mess.

"We're going to get you
up to the house," said Momma.

The boy was frightened.
"No! Leave me alone!
I'll get out of here
in a couple of days."

"You'll be dead
in a couple of days,"
said Momma.

The boy tried to crawl away.
"Let me go!" he whimpered.

"Listen," said Momma.
"You're some mother's child.
We'll look after you.
One day you'll go home
to your own mother."

## Chapter Six

# Fast-Beating Heart

Joshua and Momma
stood on each side
of the wounded boy.

"You hold him good, now,"
Momma told Joshua.
Mary Beth raised the lantern
to show the way.

Step by step,
they took the boy
out of the barn,
across the grass,
and into the house.

As they helped him
up the wooden stairs,
Joshua felt the boy's heart
beating fast with pain and fear.

That heartbeat felt
exactly like a drumbeat.